Testimony

Carefully Obtained and Carefully Maintained

I0808450

Testimony

Carefully Obtained and Carefully Maintained

By
Douglas J. Vermeeren

CFI
Springville, Utah

ISBN 13: 978-1-55517-996-0
ISBN 10: 1-55517-996-7

Published by CFI, an imprint of Cedar Fort, Inc., 2373 W. 700 S., Springville, UT, 84663
Distributed by Cedar Fort, Inc., www.cedarfort.com

LIBRARY OF CONGRESS CATALOGING-IN-PUBLICATION DATA

Vermeeren, Douglas J.
Testimony : carefully obtained and carefully maintained / Douglas J. Vermeeren.
p. cm.
ISBN-13: 978-1-55517-996-0
1. Witness bearing (Christianity) 2. Church of Jesus Christ of Latter-day Saints--Doctrines. 3. Mormon Church--Doctrines. I. Title.

BX8643.T45V47 2006
248'.5--dc22

2006032355

Cover design by Nicole Williams
Cover design © 2006 by Lyle Mortimer
Edited by Kammi Rencher
Typeset by Kammi Rencher

Printed in the United States of America

10 9 8 7 6 5 4 3 2 1

Printed on acid-free paper

Table of Contents

Introduction

Several weeks ago I was sitting in a fast and testimony meeting. It was similar to many testimony meetings that I have attended, and if you've been a member of the Church for any length of time, you have no doubt also participated in a meeting very similar.

As I listened, I began to realize that some thoughts expressed were powerful testimonies, while others were not really testimonies at all.

Some were feelings borne with great conviction, while others were simply stories that went on with little message. In some cases I was actually confused and really didn't know what was trying to be said. It was then that I began to realize that perhaps many in the Church do not understand what a testimony really is.

As I sat and thought about "testimony" in my own mind, I saw a young girl take her father by the hand and bring him to the pulpit. The father was there for her security as the little girl perched herself behind the microphone.

She stood for a moment in silence. Perhaps fearing that

nerves had gotten the best of her, the father leaned over and whispered in the little girl's ear.

But she didn't need any help and quickly reminded him she was there for her own reasons. "I'm trying to grow my own testimony," she said.

This was instructional to me. It put the concept of testimony into a more proper perspective. I had heard many varieties of testimonies, thank-imonies, and story-monies, and this young girl had summed it all up: all of these expressions are ways in which people are growing their own testimonies.

As I thought on this lesson, I was reminded of several scriptures and statements from the brethren on testimony. In my missionary days, I had been admonished to "open [my] mouth" (D&C 28:16), and to "declare the things which [I] have heard, and verily believe, and know to be true" (D&C 80:4). Another example can be found in President Packer's famous testimony talk, "Candle of the Lord," when he says that "a testimony is found in the bearing of it."

I began to feel like I had a long way to go with my own testimony, and that perhaps I should spend some serious time studying, pondering, and listening to the Spirit to discover what a testimony really is and how it is grown and maintained. As I have pursued this course I have been overwhelmed and impressed with an idea that I have since developed into a simple slogan:

Testimony—carefully obtained and carefully maintained.

I have assembled the results of my search into this short book in hopes that it might help others to follow the path to testimony or to strengthen their convictions of what they already know to be true.

Joseph Smith expressed the importance of testimony when he said:

> "The fundamental principles of our religion are the *testimonies* of the Apostles and Prophets, concerning Jesus Christ, that He died, was buried, and rose again the third day, and ascending into heaven; and all other things which pertain to our religion are only appendages to it"[1] (emphasis added).

Most of the time this scripture is discussed to teach the importance of the Atonement. But I think we are only getting half the message. What Joseph Smith is also saying is that the fundamental principle of our religion is directly connected to testimony.

We must not underestimate the importance of testimony.

In fact, Joseph Smith stated in his personal history that it was "testimony of James" (see JS–H 1:26) that inspired him to pursue the course of action that led to the First Vision.

In John 17:3, the Savior spoke of the importance of obtaining a testimony when he said, "And this is life eternal, that they might *know* thee the only true God, and Jesus Christ, whom thou hast sent" (emphasis added).

In the Doctrine and Covenants we are admonished to "declare the things which ye have heard, and verily believe, and know to be true" (D&C 80:4).

This knowledge is testimony. It is a gift from God and can only come as one pursues the pattern established for gaining, maintaining, and developing a testimony.

Or, as the little girl in the meeting called it, "growing your own testimony."

Joseph Smith also stated,

> "A man is saved no faster than he gets knowledge, for if he does not get knowledge, he will be brought into captivity by some evil power in the other world, as evil spirits have more knowledge and consequently more power than many men who are on the earth. Hence it

> needs revelation to assist us, and give us knowledge of the things of God."[2]

Thus, to be saved in the celestial kingdom a person needs a testimony, which is a knowledge of the things of God.

As you will soon see, this pattern requires commitment, diligence, obedience, and seeking after the Spirit. For we read in Revelation 19:10 that "the testimony of Jesus is the spirit of prophecy." To have the spirit of prophecy enter into our lives requires bringing our lives into harmony with the things that invite the Spirit. And that's why I want to share my slogan once again:

Testimony—carefully obtained and carefully maintained.

NOTES

1. Smith, Joseph. *Teachings of the Prophet Joseph Smith.* Selected by Joseph Fielding Smith. (Salt Lake City: Deseret Book, 1976), 121.
2. ibid, 217.

Chapter I

The Importance of a Testimony

A few years ago I spent a year as a teacher in communist China. It was one of the greatest experiences of my life. I loved the people and I loved the country.

As I went to leave China from the Beijing airport, I took my airplane ticket and headed for the departure gates.

My first stop was a government customs station. The female inspector reached out for my documents and quickly flipped through them. She paused. Something was missing. In broken English she tried to explain the problem. "Foreign expert certificate card?"

I shrugged.

She asked again, "Foreign expert certificate card?"

I must have looked at her like I had no idea what she meant. She tried to explain.

"You do not have correct documentation to leave country."

Together we carefully looked through my documents again and found she was right. I was missing documentation. Without it, I would not be permitted to leave the country.

I became a little bit concerned as she called over additional customs officers to try to find a solution. After several minutes of deliberation, it was decided that I really didn't look Chinese; I was indeed a Canadian citizen and could be allowed to return home.

It was a frightening experience, but also an instructive one.

In the scriptures we read that certain requirements, just like documents, are also necessary to return to the presence of our Heavenly Father.

One of these requirements is to receive a testimony of Jesus. This means we must hear, accept, act on, and improve our testimonies. The scriptures say many things that would indicate clearly that a testimony must also be in the possession of the individual, allowing the person to overcome all things (see D&C 76:51–60).

Jesus also describes the necessity of having this knowledge of God and himself in order to obtain eternal life, which is to live in God's presence.

Not only is testimony a requirement, it is also a responsibility of all who are baptized.

> Yea, and are *willing to...stand as witnesses* of God at all times and in all things, and in all places that ye may be in, even until death, that ye may be redeemed of God, and be numbered with those of the first resurrection, that ye may have eternal life. (Mosiah 18:9; emphasis added)

The Prophet Joseph Smith also stated, "Whenever salvation has been administered, it has been by testimony."[1]

Testimony begins with being a willing witness and ends with having a personal knowledge that permits entrance into the presence of the Father. Testimony is a principle of power. Having a testimony gives us strength to resist and overcome the adversary, brings us closer to God, brings unity, softens hearts, and converts to Christ.

Satan also recognizes the importance of testimony. One of his first attacks on the gospel in this dispensation was on Joseph Smith's testimony.

After the First Vision, Joseph bore his testimony. Satan tried to persecute and intimidate young Joseph by turning many in the community against him. It was Satan's hope that if he could stop Joseph from feeling right about what he knew, that perhaps he might just forget it ever happened.

Can you imagine the strength it would take for a fourteen-year-old boy to maintain his testimony under such circumstances?

Joseph writes about his experiences after the vision, saying,

> I soon found, however, that my telling the story had excited a great deal of prejudice against me among professors of religion, and was the cause of great persecution, which continued to increase; and though I was an obscure boy, only between fourteen and fifteen years of age, and my circumstances in life such as to make a boy of no consequence in the world, yet men of high standing would take notice sufficient to excite the public mind against me, and create a bitter persecution; and this was common among all the sects—all united to persecute me.
>
> It caused me serious reflection then, and often has since, how very strange it was that an obscure boy, of a little over fourteen years of age, and one, too, who was doomed to the necessity of obtaining a scanty maintenance by his daily labor, should be thought a character of sufficient importance to attract the attention of the great ones of the most popular sects of the day, and in a manner to create in them a spirit of the most bitter

> persecution and reviling. But strange or not, so it was, and it was often the cause of great sorrow to myself.
>
> However, it was nevertheless a fact that I had beheld a vision. I have thought since, that I felt much like Paul, when he made his defense before King Agrippa, and related the account of the vision he had when he saw a light, and heard a voice; but still there were but few who believed him; some said he was dishonest, others said he was mad; and he was ridiculed and reviled. But all this did not destroy the reality of his vision. He had seen a vision, he knew he had, and all the persecution under heaven could not make it otherwise; and though they should persecute him unto death, yet he knew, and would know to his latest breath, that he had both seen a light and heard a voice speaking unto him, and all the world could not make him think or believe otherwise.
>
> So it was with me. I had actually seen a light, and in the midst of that light I saw two Personages, and they did in reality speak to me; and though I was hated and persecuted for saying that I had seen a vision, yet it was true; and while they were persecuting me, reviling me, and speaking all manner of evil against me falsely for so saying, I was led to say in my heart: Why persecute me for telling the truth? I have actually seen a vision; and who am I that I can withstand God, or why does the world think to make me deny what I have actually seen? For I had seen a vision; I knew it, and I knew that God knew it, and I could not deny it, neither dared I do it; at least I knew that by so doing I would offend God, and come under condemnation. (JS–H 1:22–25)

When Satan discovered he could not shake Joseph's testimony, he tried another tactic. As Joseph Smith and Martin Harris were translating the Book of Mormon, Martin lost 116 pages of the manuscript. Inquiring of the Lord on how to proceed under these challenging circumstances,

Joseph received the following instruction, which identified Satan's desires: "Thus Satan thinketh to overpower your testimony in this generation, that the work may not come forth in this generation" (D&C 10:33).

Satan's real desire had little to do with stealing parts of the Book of Mormon manuscript. He no doubt knew that Heavenly Father was prepared for this difficulty. Satan's real desires were to destroy Joseph's testimony. Satan knew that without Joseph's testimony, the work could be hindered in our day.

The Church still uses testimony to fight Satan today. Joseph Anderson, who served as an assistant to the twelve Apostles, wrote:

> The strength of this church does not depend alone upon the prophets and apostles of earlier dispensations nor upon the testimony of the General Authorities of the present. The strength of this church is in the testimony and faith of its members, and every member may have that testimony if he will seek it through study and sincere prayer and if he will keep the commandments the Lord has given us.[2]

Testimony has always been a source of great strength against Satan, both for the Church and for individuals. A testimony can lift us and sustain us in all of our troubles and challenges, both spiritually and physically.

But in the same way Satan attacks us, so must our defence be:individual.

Elder Heber C. Kimball once expressed the importance of individual testimony when he said:

> Let me say to you, that many of you will see the time when you will have all the trouble, trial, and persecution that you can stand, and plenty of opportunities to show that you are true to God and his work. This Church has

> before it many close places through which it will have to pass before the work of God is crowned with victory.
>
> The time will come when *no man nor woman will be able to endure on borrowed light.* Each will have to be guided by the light within himself. If you do not have it, how can you stand?[3] (emphasis added)

Elder James E. Faust also commented on the importance of individual testimony when he said, "Each of us has to receive our own witness concerning Jesus as the Christ. We cannot get it second hand from someone else."[4]

The Savior said it another way in the parable of the ten virgins. You'll remember that only five out of the ten virgins had enough oil in their lamps when called to meet the bride groom. They could not borrow oil from another at that time. They could only rely on what they had brought. Testimony is the same. Although we can exist for a time on borrowed light, we must eventually have our own light with our own oil or we will be shut out in outer darkness. (See Matthew 25)

In another parable, the Savior said we must let our own light shine before the world. We cannot accomplish this with borrowed light; we must have our own light first. (See Matthew 5:16)

In addition to these principle reasons for acquiring and maintaining a testimony, there are other reasons which are also important. "Nevertheless, ye are blessed, for the testimony which ye have borne is recorded in heaven for the angels to look upon; and they rejoice over you, and your sins are forgiven you" (D&C 62:3). Blessings and forgiveness come as gifts to those who bear testimony. Both are needed in the daily lives of Latter-day saints.

Testimony is not only a valuable treasure in this life, but it will also be a valuable treasure to us throughout eternity.

President Ezra Taft Benson said, "A testimony is one of the few possessions we may take with us when we leave this life."[5]

The Doctrine and Covenants describes it this way: "Whatever principle of intelligence we attain unto in this life, it will rise with us in the resurrection" (D&C 130:18). Testimony can be ours and it will be eternal. It can be our most precious gift. It can be our support through mortal struggles and a protective armor against the efforts of the adversary.

Notes

1. Smith, Joseph. *Teachings of the Prophet Joseph Smith.* Selected by Joseph Fielding Smith. (Salt Lake City: Deseret Book, 1976), 121.
2. Joseph Anderson, "The Matter of Personal Testimony," *Ensign,* May 1976, 87.
3. Whitney, Orson F. *Life of Heber C. Kimball, an Apostle.* (Salt Lake City: Kimball Family, 1888), 449–450.
4. James E. Faust, "A Testimony of Christ," *Liahona,* March 2005, 3.
5. Ezra Taft Benson, "Valiant n the Testimony of Jesus," *Ensign,* February 1987, 2.

Chapter 2
The Elements of a Testimony

"Do you swear to tell the truth, the whole truth and nothing but the truth?" Isn't that what they say in a court of law? "Nine out of ten doctors prefer our medical miracle to other leading brands." Isn't that what you hear on TV?

From the perspective of the world, a testimony is often used to prove a point or to endorse a certain way of thinking. In a court of law testimony can be used to establish the truth of a matter. In the advertising world a testimonial can be used to try to convince someone to use a new product or service.

In the gospel context a testimony can serve both to establish truth and to convince. But a testimony of the gospel is also so much more.

I love words. I love understanding where they come from and what they mean. Often in my personal study of the gospel I spend effort investigating words that define or are related to the concepts I am trying to understand. As I did this with "testimony," I found a very interesting list of words. These have helped to define what a testimony of the gospel is. I believe they are worth sharing. Here are the words: statement, evidence, acknowledgement, declaration, witness, proof, authentication, deposition, report, avowal, testimonial, proclamation, account, affirmation, verification, confirmation, corroboration, impervious, tribute, confession, pledge, participant, certification, endorsement, affidavit, observer, onlooker, warning.

I'd like to examine these words in more detail. Consider how they might apply to testimony in a gospel setting.

Statement—A concise, well thought out collection of words committed either verbally or in writing.

Evidence—A set of tangible facts, figures, items, or situations which support an idea.

Acknowledgment—The act of recognizing and admitting a fact or situation.

Declaration—A statement of truth made with boldness.

Authentication—A truth supported by evidence or qualified experts.

Deposition—Testimony under oath, especially a statement by a witness that is recorded for use at a later date.

Report—A recital of events.

Avowal—A frank admission or acknowledgement.

Testimonial—A statement in support of a particular truth, fact, or claim.

Tribute—Something given in appreciation of a person's service or achievement; to cite the goodness of another.

Proclamation—A published declaration.

Account—A detailed report. Consider that the words "accounting" and "accountant" come from this word.

Affirmation/certification—Standing behind or sustaining the truth of a matter.

Verification/Corroboration—A secondary witness, proof, or evidence of a particular truth.

Confirmation—Making solid. Literally means "with firmness."

Impervious—Without defect, cannot be disputed or held in question.

Confession—To share one's faults, declare one's beliefs, or request support.

Endorsement—To give one's name to support an idea, fact, or belief.

Affidavit/pledge—A statement under oath to the truth of a matter before an authorized officer.

Observer/witness/onlooker/participant—One who knows by firsthand experience. Typically this is the result of one of the five senses.

Warning—To share with others a learned principle so that they may in turn learn to avoid future challenges or painful situations for themselves.

We can see examples of these as we closely examine the testimonies borne in the scriptures and by our present-day General Authorities.

While the way testimonies are borne and shared may have reflections in worldly terminology, the way that testimonies are obtained and shared is very far from worldly understanding. A testimony is a gift from God.

We read in Doctrine and Covenants 46:13–14:

> To some it is given by the Holy Ghost to know that Jesus Christ is the Son of God, and that he was crucified for the sins of the world. To others it is given to believe on their words, that they also might have eternal life if they continue faithful. (emphasis added)

A testimony is a clear declaration of things which only the Host Ghost can teach and only the Holy Ghost can confirm.

In trying to define what testimony is we should also discuss what it is not. I would like to share a story from Elder Boyd K. Packer:

> I had an experience in the mission field that taught me much about testimony. In spite of the fact that all seemed to be under control, we were not progressing as we should. It was not something we were doing that we ought not to do so much, I felt, as something we were not doing that we ought to be doing.
>
> We held a series of zone conferences to improve the spirituality in the mission. Rather than schedule instruction on the mechanics of missionary work, we determined to have a testimony meeting. In the last conference, in the testimony of one of the humble elders, I found the answer to the problem. There was something different about the brief testimony of this frightened new elder. He stood for less than a minute, yet I learned from his expression what it was that was missing.
>
> The testimonies we'd heard from all the other missionaries went something like this: "I'm grateful to be in the mission field. I've learned a lot from it. I have a fine companion. I've learned a lot from him. I'm grateful for my parents. We had an interesting experience last week. We were out knocking on doors and ..." Then the missionary would relate an experience. His conclusion would be something like this: "I'm grateful to be in the mission field. I have a testimony of the gospel." And he would conclude "in the name of Jesus Christ. Amen."
>
> This young elder was different somehow. Anxious not to spend an extra second on his feet, he said simply, in hurried, frightened words, "I know that God lives. I know that Jesus is the Christ. I know that we have

> a prophet of God leading the Church. In the name of Jesus Christ. Amen."
>
> This was a testimony. It was not just an experience nor an expression of gratitude. It was a declaration, a witness!
>
> Most of the elders had said "I have a testimony," but they had not declared it. This young elder had, in a very few words, delivered his testimony—direct, basic, and, as it turned out, powerful.
>
> I then knew what was wrong in the mission. We were telling stories, expressing gratitude, admitting that we had testimonies, but we were not bearing them.[1]

Testimonies are not stories. Testimonies are not public expressions of thanks or love. Testimonies are not an exhortation or a sermon. Testimonies are also not the relating of an experience, although experiences may be used to illustrate a belief or conviction. Testimonies are not a public confession of sins.

In short, testimony is not a long explanation of how you know, but rather a witness of what you know.

Elder M. Russell Ballard of the quorum of the Twelve apostles adds this insight:

> We often hear some members, and especially children, bear their testimonies, listing things for which they are thankful: their love of family, the Church, their teachers, their friends. For them, the gospel is something that they are grateful for because it makes them feel happy and secure. This is a *good beginning,* but testimonies need to be much more. They need to be anchored very early to the first principles of the gospel.[2] (emphasis added)

As I have sought to understand testimony I have been impressed by the number of times that the brethren have mentioned this. Elder Ballard continues:

> Our testimony meetings need to be more centered on the Savior, the doctrines of the gospel, the blessings of the Restoration, and the teachings of the scriptures. We need to replace stories, travelogues, and lectures with pure testimonies. Those who are entrusted to speak and teach in our meetings need to do so with doctrinal power that will be both heard and felt, lifting the spirits and edifying our people.[3]

President Howard W. Hunter issued another warning that we should also consider carefully. He stated,

> I get concerned when it appears that strong emotion or free-flowing tears are equated with the presence of the Spirit. Certainly the Spirit of the Lord can bring strong emotional feelings, including tears, but that outward manifestation ought not to be confused with the presence of the Spirit itself.[4]

We must be careful not to always equate emotion with the presence of the Spirit. The Holy Ghost brings a refining spirit. His efforts and actions will always be calculated to draw us nearer to God and make us more like Him. We should seek to have this refining spirit in our testimonies.

A testimony is not a free gift. When people investigate or join the Church, they are not always automatically given the gift of a testimony. Like all other gospel blessings, testimonies are awarded as one complies with the principles that govern that particular blessing. (See D&C 130:20–21)

A testimony is a gift from God with a great responsibility attached. When we understand what it really is, a testimony will change our lives. A testimony will draw us closer to our Heavenly Father and help us return to live with Him again.

Notes

1. Packer, Boyd K. *Teach Ye Diligently,* rev. ed. (Salt Lake City: Deseret Book, 1993), 323–24.
2. M. Russell Ballard, "Pure Testimony," *Ensign,* November 2004, 40.
3. ibid, 40.
4. Hunter, Howard W. *The Teachings of Howard W. Hunter.* Edited by Clyde J. Williams. (Salt Lake City: Bookcraft, 1997), 184.

CHAPTER 3

Gaining a Testimony

How do you gain a testimony? This is a question that is addressed often in the scriptures and by modern day General Authorities. The journey to increased testimony has been described as a "divinely appointed process," "a pattern," "a course," "qualifying steps," and more.

The more I looked at the descriptions of this process, the more it reminded me of another word: equation.

When I was in the third grade I wasn't a very good math student. I found math confusing and often times difficult to understand. I remember the day when my teacher came to the chalkboard with a new concept. She wrote the number three on the board, left a space, and then wrote the number five across from it. She then asked, "Is three greater than five?"

The students at first weren't sure what she meant. She rephrased the question. "Is three more than five?"

"No," we all answered in unison.

She then put a symbol between the numbers and the equation looked like this: $3 < 5$.

She then asked about another set of numbers.

"Is 6 greater than 2?"

This time we were all starting to get it.

"Yes!" We shouted out.

"Good." She wrote the equation as 6 > 2.

She then explained that you can think of the arrow symbol to be like the mouth of a fish. It always goes after the greater number.

Then she had one that stumped us. She wrote on the board 8 and then 8. We looked at each other some of us shrugged. "They are the same," a boy shouted out.

The teacher nodded and wrote in the equal symbol: 8 = 8.

She then explained that = was called the equal symbol.

Later in life I had another math teacher explain it as follows: "The symbol = is generally used to express a statement asserting the equality of two expressions, usually written as a linear array of symbols that are separated into left and right sides of a problem."

What?

Putting it into regular people terms, when you see the equal symbol, it means both sides are the same.

So, you're probably wondering how this applies to testimony.

How a testimony is gained is also an equation. The degree that that individual complies with the laws of testimony = the witness that the Holy Ghost will provide towards that testimony.

An equation or promise like this is also called a covenant. Thus, a testimony is obtained in a covenant formula.

This idea is nothing new. Have you ever looked closely at the Gospels in the New Testaments? In the footnotes, we can see that the Prophet Joseph Smith called the Gospels "testimonies." It was the compilers of these testimonies that called the collection of testimonies the "New Testament," meaning "new covenant."

In Matthew 7:7–8, the Savior explained what is required by the individual to gain a testimony:

> Ask, and it shall be given you; seek, and ye shall find; knock, and it shall be opened unto you: For every one that asketh recieveth; and he that seekth findeth; and to him that knocketh it shall be opened.

The promise is that if we do these things we will receive, find, and have answers opened to us from our Heavenly Father through the Holy Ghost. That is the equation. Moroni states the equation another way: "for ye receive no witness until after the trial of your faith" (Ether 12:6).

I'd like to look at each of the elements of the equation separately to understand better what is required of us and what blessings can be expected from the Holy Ghost in return.

But before I do, I want to clearly state that these principles are not one-time steps. Each of these principles must always be present and always work with each other in order to gain and maintain a testimony.

Individual Effort

All things begin with the individual. President Brigham Young stated,

> Let every one get a knowledge for himself that this work is true. We do not want you to say that it is true until you know that it is; and if you know it, that knowledge is as good to you as though the Lord came down and told you.[1]

Testimonies are not obtained accidentally. Testimonies are obtained by those who desire and are carefully seeking to know.

Alma writes,

> But behold, if ye will awake and arouse your faculties, even to an experiment upon my words, and exercise even a particle of faith, yea, even if ye can no more than desire to believe, let this desire work in you, even until ye can give place for a portion of my words. (Alma 32:27)

Moroni talks about the nature of this desire: "and if ye shall ask with a sincere heart, with real intent…" (see Moroni 10:4). In James 1:5–6 similar language is used when James says "nothing wavering."

Desire, commitment, humility, real intent, nothing wavering— these are required for a testimony and all these things begin with the individual.

I spoke not too long ago with an associate of mine about how a person can know the things of God. He was curious about why I believed what I do. As we discussed the subject he made several positive comments and told me he was beginning to understand. I thought I was sitting on a golden missionary opportunity.

I asked him if he would be interested to know more. That's when he said something bizarre: "Oh I'm not really that interested. I'm just curious. I don't really want to make any commitments to anybody."

When we consider how life changing a testimony is, simply being curious is not enough to get answers. Answers of eternal significance will only come to us when we are committed to following God and put forth the effort to do so.

Pray

The commandment to pray is given more often in scripture than is any other commandment. In the process of gaining and maintaining a testimony, prayer is essential and it cannot be a one time event. We are commanded in the scriptures to "pray often" or "pray without ceasing." Joseph Smith once stated that a person "cannot pray too much."[2] Without prayer, testimonies cannot be obtained nor sustained.

Much could be said about prayer. All humble, honest, and sincere prayers that are offered in the name of Jesus Christ will be answered. The more carefully we pray and prepare to pray, the more clear our answers may become. When we pray for significant spiritual understanding, we must "stretch ourselves" spiritually.

Fasting is a valuable tool in bringing our prayers into harmony with these attributes. In gaining his testimony, Alma the Younger stated,

> Behold, I say unto you they are made known unto me by the Holy Spirit of God. Behold, I have *fasted and prayed many days* that I might know these things of myself. And now I do know of myself that they are true; for the Lord God hath made them manifest unto me by his Holy Spirit; and this is the spirit of revelation which is in me. (Alma 5:46; emphasis added)

We must pray in the proper spirit and setting. We must also choose times and locations where we can devote our focus to spiritual things, since reverence invites revelation. Answers will come as we are ready to receive them. Sometimes this will be done on the spot with a marvellous manifestation. More often testimony will grow slowly—sometimes so slowly that it can be unrecognizable.

It is interesting to note in the above experience that although Alma had seen an angel, his testimony came to him over "many days." Elder Richard G. Scott helps us understand this process. "A powerful testimony distils from quiet moments of prayer and pondering as you recognize the impressions that will accompany such effort."[3]

In reaching prayer of this type, vain repetitions and insincerity fade away and are replaced with a longing desire to know.

Prayer is essential to testimony and to understanding the gospel. When Nephi's brothers Laman and Lemuel could not understand the Lord's words, the first question Nephi asked them was related to prayer. "Have ye inquired of the Lord?" (1 Nephi 15:8)

In regards to learning spiritual truth, Joseph Smith stated, "The best way to obtain truth and wisdom is not to ask it from books, but to go to God in prayer, and obtain divine teaching."[4] The Lord will provide answers when a humble heart is ready to listen and obey.

Plant the Seed

Imagine a farmer in an open field.

He selected his spot carefully. Satisfied, he began to work. He carefully ploughed, prepared, and cultivated the lands. Next, he watered everything carefully. He continued to nurture the land and remove weeds and other obstacles to growth. He had done all that he could to ensure success. The weather was great and there was no reason why he shouldn't be successful.

But he failed. Why?

He did everything but plant the seeds. Without seeds, nothing can grow.

The prophet Alma compares the process of gaining a testimony to the growing of a seed. He states,

> Now, we will compare the word unto a seed. Now, if ye give place, that a seed may be planted in your heart, behold, if it be a true seed, or a good seed, if ye do not cast it out by your unbelief, that ye will resist the Spirit of the Lord, behold, it will begin to swell within your breasts; and when you feel these swelling motions, ye will begin to say within yourselves—It must needs be that this is a good seed, or that the word is good, for it beginneth to enlarge my soul; yea, it beginneth to enlighten my understanding, yea, it beginneth to be delicious to me. (Alma 32:28)

The seed is the Word. Consider the analogy of the farmer—nothing will grow unless the word or seed is present.

How do we plant the seed?

Jesus identified a method for planting the seed. "Search the scriptures; for in them ye think ye have eternal life: and they are they which testify of me" (John 5:39). In the Doctrine & Covenants we also read,

> These words are not of men nor of man, but of me; wherefore, you shall testify they are of me and not of man; For it is my voice which speaketh them unto you; for they are given by my Spirit unto you, and by my power you can read them one to another; and save it were by my power you could not have them; Wherefore, you can testify that you have heard my voice, and know my words. (D&C 18:34–36)

Not only is the written text of the scriptures the word of God, but also the words of living Prophets and Apostles when they are speaking the mind and will of the Lord. "Whether by mine own voice or by the voice of my servants, it is the same." (D&C 1:38)

As we listen to the words the Lord's prophets and apostles we are planting the seed.

In acquiring testimony, it is important to learn the lesson of the parable of the sower. Jesus shared the parable and then explained it:

> And he spake many things unto them in parables, saying, Behold, a sower went forth to sow; And when he sowed, some seeds fell by the way side, and the fowls came and devoured them up: Some fell upon stony places, where they had not much earth: and forthwith they sprung up, because they had no deepness of earth: And when the sun was up, they were scorched; and because they had no root, they withered away. And some fell among thorns; and the thorns sprung up, and choked them: But other fell into good ground, and brought forth fruit, some an hundredfold, some sixtyfold, some thirtyfold. Who hath ears to hear, let him hear. (Matthew 13:3–9)
>
> Hear ye therefore the parable of the sower. When any one heareth the word of the kingdom, and understandeth it not, then cometh the wicked one, and catcheth away that which was sown in his heart. This is he which received seed by the way side. But he that received the seed into stony places, the same is he that heareth the word, and anon with joy receiveth it; Yet hath he not root in himself, but dureth for a while: for when tribulation or persecution ariseth because of the word, by and by he is offended. He also that received seed among the thorns is he that heareth the word; and the care of this world, and the deceitfulness of riches, choke the word, and he becometh unfruitful.
>
> But he that received seed into the good ground is he that heareth the word, and understandeth it; which also beareth fruit, and bringeth forth, some an hundredfold, some sixty, some thirty. (Matthew 13:18–23)

It is not enough to have the word alone. A seed placed in a bad environment is not well prepared to survive. It will not grow.

Leaning on the word alone, with only our own understanding to guide us, will not bring us a knowledge of the things of God. Our own understanding cannot create the gift of testimony. We may endure for a season but by and by in the heat of the day we will find that our roots are not be deep enough, and our efforts will be fruitless.

It is important to remember that for the seed to grow it must also be constantly nourished and revisited. A planting followed by neglect will not yield fruit. Alma shares the results of nourishing the seed:

> And thus, if ye will not nourish the word, looking forward with an eye of faith to the fruit thereof, ye can never pluck of the fruit of the tree of life. But if ye will nourish the word, yea, nourish the tree as it beginneth to grow, by your faith with great diligence, and with patience, looking forward to the fruit thereof, it shall take root; and behold it shall be a tree springing up unto everlasting life. (Alma 32:40–41)

Again we see how carefully testimony is connected to eternal and everlasting life.

It is important to remember that ignorance is a roadblock to progression.

Walk

When I was in the second grade I played in our community flag football league. I wasn't a football star by any means. In fact, I had a few embarrassing moments—not because I wasn't athletic, but because I didn't really understand the game.

I remember one such game. It was one of my first. The game had just started and the coach sent me out to play. The ball was set down on the grass then our team gathered in a huddle. One of the boys with a lot more experience conducted our brief meeting. I thought this group discussion was pretty interesting, but when it finished I started to return to the bench to sit with the coach.

I still remember everyone trying to direct me back out to the field. "Go play." I stopped, turned around, and saw all the other boys line up to put the ball in play. Then I remembered, "Oh yes. We are supposed to be playing now." I was pretty embarrassed.

The principle of walking is much like the experience I have just related. I met with the team, and listened to the game plan, but I didn't head out onto the field to play the game. Likewise, we can listen in Church, and discuss doctrine, but unless we are actually living the gospel, applying the principles we learn in our lives, we fail to "walk." Without the follow up principle of action, a search for a testimony will yield no productive fruit.

The actions that are required for gaining and keeping a testimony are obedience, diligence, and perseverance. One of my favorite scriptures in the entire Book of Mormon is possibly one of the most camouflaged jewels in the book. It's a special verse that holds a great key in a single word—but often remains invisible until it is pointed out. In the very first chapter of the Book of Mormon, Lehi has a vision. And in the vision he is presented a special book. Nephi writes about his father's experience: "And it came to pass that as he read, he was filled with the Spirit of the Lord" (1 Nephi 1:12).

There is a key in that verse to testimony. It is the word "as." Testimonies are found as we obey.

The Savior also makes clear this principle when he said, "If any man will *do* his will, he shall know of the doctrine, whether it be of God, or *whether* I speak of myself" (John 7:17; emphasis added).

Brigham Young said it even more clearly: "More testimonies are gained on our feet than on our knees."[5] Obedience allows the Holy Ghost to put His stamp of approval on a principle. When we receive this approval by the Holy Ghost, we become personal firsthand witnesses and can bear testimony. "And we are his witnesses of these things; and so is also the Holy Ghost, whom God hath given to them that obey him" (Acts 5:32).

Part of being obedient includes repenting of our sins. Sins can keep the whisperings of the Holy Ghost from being heard and understood. It is instructional to note the wording given when a person is confirmed a member of the Church. They are told to receive the Holy Ghost, not the other way around. The Holy Ghost is not commanded to receive us. We must make ourselves ready.

President Marion G. Romney gave some important counsel:

> It is the mission of the Holy Ghost to reveal the truth of heaven to those who qualify to receive it. Every one of us, if we will, may so qualify. We must keep in mind, however, that he will not dwell in an unholy environment. He is used to society of God, for he is an associate of the Father and the Son. When we receive the gift of the Holy Ghost, we are commanded to receive him; he is not commanded to come to us. But if, with all our hearts, we truly seek him, he will come unto us and guide us in the making of decisions at every crisis of our lives.[6]

We must make the first step to prepare ourselves for

heavenly things. This process is clear through out the scriptures.

We read in the Doctrine and Covenants that the Lord is always ready to come to us as soon as we are ready to receive him. "Draw near unto me and I will draw near unto you; seek me diligently and ye shall find me; ask, and ye shall receive; knock, and it shall be opened unto you" (D&C 88:63).

President David O. McKay taught,

> "A testimony of the gospel of Jesus Christ is the most sacred, the most precious gift in our lives, obtained only by adherence to the principles of the gospel, not by following the paths of the world."[7]

Obedience demonstrates our desire to move toward our Heavenly Father and confirms our willingness to follow the Lord. "Be thou humble, and the Lord thy God shall lead thee by the hand, and give thee answer to thy prayers" (D&C 112:10). We are not told that the Lord will carry us to our answers. We will be led. In order to be lead we must be prepared to move our feet.

Bear Your Testimony

There is another important part of walking. That is to actually make that leap of faith and bear your testimony. President Boyd K. Packer spoke of this when he said,

> A testimony is found in the bearing of it. Somewhere in your quest for spiritual knowledge, there is that "leap of faith," as the philosophers call it. It is the moment when you have gone to the edge of the light and step into the darkness to discover that the way is lighted ahead for just a footstep or two.[8]

This same promise of finding spiritual knowledge

and testimony by bearing it is given in the Doctrine and Covenants.

> The time has verily come that it is necessary and expedient in me that you should open your mouths in proclaiming my gospel, the things of the kingdom, expounding the mysteries thereof out of the scriptures, according to that portion of Spirit and power which shall be given unto you, even as I will. (D&C 71:1; see also D&C 33:8,10)

Bearing testimony is one way of putting to action the principle of walking.

The Witness of the Holy Ghost

Up until now all the aspects of this recipe have been provided by the individual. The balance of the testimony equation comes as a gift from the Holy Ghost. We often take the Holy Ghost for granted. I know I have shared this quote before but I want to share a part of it again to emphasize something so important. President Marion G. Romney, speaking of the Holy Ghost, said, "We must keep in mind, however, that he will not dwell in an unholy environment. He is used to society of God, for he is an associate of the Father and the Son."[9]

For the witness of this member of the godhead to come to us we must be carefully prepared.

In 1 Kings we read of Elijah's experience with the Spirit:

> And, behold, the Lord passed by, and a great and strong wind rent the mountains, and brake in pieces the rocks before the Lord; but the Lord was not in the wind: and after the wind an earthquake; but the Lord was not in the earthquake: And after the earthquake a fire; but

> the Lord was not in the fire: and after the fire a still small voice. (1 Kings 19:11–12)

The Holy Ghost speaks by a still small voice that can only be discerned by those who are prepared to hear it.

Consider this:

Still—Calming; John 14:26 also uses the word "comforter."

Small—Whisper. If you aren't paying attention you will miss it.

Voice—Clear and precise. Not an inaudible noise, but a distinct sound.

About this voice President Joseph Fielding Smith said,

> The impressions on the soul that come from the Holy Ghost are far more significant than a vision. It is where Spirit speaks to spirit, and the imprint upon the soul is far more difficult to erase. Every member of the Church should have the impressions on his soul made by the Holy Ghost that Jesus is the Son of God indelibly pictured so that they cannot be forgotten.[10]

In John 14:26 the Savior reveals a key to understanding truth revealed from the Holy Ghost. He calls the Holy Ghost the comforter; that means when the Holy Ghost is speaking, it feels comfortable. This is expressed another way in Doctrine and Covenants 9:8 when the Lord says that if something is right, "you shall feel that it is right."

In addition to recognizing truth, another important mission of the Holy Ghost is to help us internalize eternal truth. In the scriptures we often hear the Holy Ghost referred to in this capacity as the "Spirit of Promise." It is by this function of the Holy Ghost that ordinances and righteous principles are sealed to us and bound to our hearts. (See Ephesians 1:13; D&C 76:53; D&C 88:3)

Nephi described this role of the Holy Ghost when he wrote: "For when a man speaketh by the power of the Holy Ghost the power of the Holy Ghost carrieth it unto the hearts of the children of men" (2 Nephi 33:1). Growing a testimony requires recognizing these moments.

A burning in the bosom may occur initially as well. But more often it is a still small voice whispering to a listening heart that something is comfortable or right. As a person listens to the Holy Ghost and obeys His promptings, the feelings will intensify.

Elder Joseph B. Wirthlin shared this insight:

> A testimony of the truth of the gospel does not come the same way to all people. Some receive it in a unique, life-changing experience. Others gain a testimony slowly, almost imperceptibly until, one day, they simply know.[11]

The process outlined by the Lord is this: "That which is of God is light; and he that receiveth light, and continueth in God, receiveth more light; and that light groweth brighter and brighter until the perfect day" (D&C 50:24).

Moroni talked about the result of this process: "And by the power of the Holy Ghost ye may know the truth of all things" (Moroni 10:5). The Holy Ghost will eventually lead us to understand all things pertaining to God and his kingdom.

Consider some of the marvellous things revealed throughout the scriptures to people like Moses, Abraham, Isaiah, John the Revelator, Joseph Smith, and others. This is the kind of understanding that the Holy Ghost will provide to all who follow this course.

Not All to Be Revealed at Once

The daily intake of water for a person should be approximately 2 liters (1/2 gallon) for the human body to function correctly. Can you imagine if you tried to drink your year's supply all in one day? What effect would that have? Certainly it would not be positive. In fact, it could be quite harmful.

Learning the gospel is similar. Our capacity will not allow us to receive everything all at once. The gospel is taught line upon line. Because learning the gospel takes time, the learner must also learn patience. For a testimony to be valuable it must be gained in the way Isaiah states:

"For precept must be upon precept, precept upon precept; line upon line, line upon line; here a little, and there a little" (Isaiah 28:10). Gaining a testimony is a process.

A testimony given by the Holy Spirit is one of the most valuable possessions we can acquire in mortality. As we strive to listen to the promptings of the Spirit, our testimony will grow until we can declare with boldness that we know clearly, without doubt, that Jesus is the Christ, the Church of Jesus Christ is His kingdom once again upon the earth, that a living prophet guides His Church, and that the Book of Mormon is another testament of Jesus Christ.

Notes

1. Young, Brigham. *Teachings of the Presidents of the Church: Brigham Young.* (Salt Lake City: The Church of Jesus Christ of Latter-day Saints, 1997), 317.
2. Smith, Joseph. *Teachings of the Prophet Joseph Smith.* Selected by Joseph Fielding Smith. (Salt Lake City: Deseret Book, 1976), 25.
3. Richard G. Scott, "The Power of a Strong Testimony," *Ensign,* November 2001, 87.
4. Smith, Joseph. *Teachings of the Prophet Joseph Smith.*

Selected by Joseph Fielding Smith. (Salt Lake City: Deseret Book, 1976), 191.

5. Brigham Young, quoted by N. Eldon Tanner, "The Power of Testimony," *Ensign,* January 1979, 3.
6. Marion G. Romney, "Revelation in Our Personal Affairs," *Relief Society Magazine,* October 1955, 647.
7. McKay, David O. *Treasures of Life,* compiled by Clare M. Middlemiss. (Salt Lake City: Deseret Book, 1962), 229.
8. Packer, Boyd K. *That All May Be Edified.* (Salt Lake City: Bookcraft, 1982), 340.
9. Marion G. Romney, "Revelation in Our Personal Affairs," *Relief Society Magazine,* October 1955, 647.
10. Smith, Joseph Fielding. *Seek Ye Earnestly.* (Salt Lake City: Deseret Book 1970), 213–14.
11. Joseph B. Wirthlin, "Pure Testimony," *Ensign,* November 2000, 22.

Chapter 4

Doubts and How to Handle Them

I want to use an analogy here. If you are reading this book in a room with a light switch in it, please stand up and go flick it off. (Go ahead—trust me, I have a point.) After you have flicked it off, go ahead and flick it on again. Try it a few times. (Warning: Don't get carried away.) I want you to now think about how that worked.

Your life experience has probably taught you that electricity travels through wires in your wall and makes the switches and bulbs work in a way that gives you light.

But do you know how that works? Do you know how electricity is generated? Do you know how it is routed to your home? Do you know how it is kept safe before getting to you? Do you know which wires are guiding it through the streets to your home? There are a lot of questions that could be asked. (And unless you are an expert in electricity you probably don't know the answers off the top of your head.)

The point I want to make is that even though we don't have all the answers it doesn't mean we cannot use a principle like electricity or make it less real. Testimony is the same. We can feel it, we can be blessed by it, we can grow it—but there may be many questions that we will never be able to answer.

President Howard W. Hunter shared the following concern:

> I have sympathy for young men and young women when honest doubts enter their minds and they engage in the great conflict of resolving doubts. These doubts can be resolved, if they have an honest desire to know the truth, by exercising moral, spiritual, and mental effort. They will emerge from the conflict into a firmer, stronger, larger faith because of the struggle. They have gone from a simple, trusting faith, through doubt and conflict, into a solid substantial faith which ripens into testimony.[1]

Doubts and questions are natural in the process of growing a testimony. Elder John K. Carmack of the first quorum of the Seventy stated:

> "Yes, I have a whole box of unanswered questions, none of them threatening to my testimony. New questions enter that box regularly. Others come out of the box, yielding to both study and experience."[2]

Questions and doubts may appear but they will not make the witness of the Spirit less real.

Not too long ago I had a discussion with a friend of mine who is not a member of the Church. He wrote me by e-mail and requested that I share how a person can know if the Church is true. After a few messages back and forth he began to bring up many things that critics of the Church have pointed out—alleged challenges with our doctrine and difficult questions from our history.

While it is true that there are many scholars in our

Church that have already answered every anti-Mormon claim, to use facts to convince him of the truth of the gospel would have been the wrong approach.

The scriptures teach that "the natural man receiveth not the things of the Spirit of God: for they are foolishness unto him: neither can he know them, because they are spiritually discerned" (1 Cor 2:14).

Without God's help man will never understand spiritual things. Man can speculate, question, criticize, and hypothesize, but he will never gain a true understanding or testimony this way.

The Book of Mormon puts it this way:

> O that cunning plan of the evil one! O the vainness, and the frailties, and the foolishness of men! When they are learned they think they are wise, and they hearken not unto the counsel of God, for they set it aside, supposing they know of themselves, wherefore, their wisdom is foolishness and it profiteth them not. And they shall perish.
>
> But to be learned is good if they hearken unto the counsels of God. (2 Nephi 9:28–29)

Jesus encountered this same challenge with the people of his day.

> When Jesus came into the coasts of Caesarea Philippi, he asked his disciples, saying, Whom do *men* say that I the Son of man am? And they said, Some say that thou art John the Baptist: some, Elias; and others, Jeremias, or one of the prophets. He saith unto them, But whom say ye that I am? And Simon Peter answered and said, Thou art the Christ, the Son of the living God.
>
> And Jesus answered and said unto him, Blessed art thou, Simon Bar-jona: for flesh and blood hath not revealed it unto thee, but my Father which is in heaven. (Matthew 16:13–17; emphasis added)

When Jesus asked what men were saying about him, he already knew that men were wrong. When Peter proclaimed the correct answer the Savior told him that it was not revealed by man—it was made known unto Peter only by the Father.

Testimony and answers to gospel questions are never given to us through debate or intellectualism. They may be strengthened by physical experiences, but obtaining spiritual answers requires something beyond that. Spiritual things can only be understood by the witness of the Holy Ghost.

While we are on the subject of addressing criticisms or doubts from non-members of the Church, the words of President Gordon B. Hinckley speak about how testimony is our greatest shield. Speaking of testimony he stated:

> It is something that cannot be refuted. Opponents may quote scripture and argue doctrine endlessly. They can be clever and persuasive. But when one says, "I know," there can be no further argument. There may not be acceptance, but who can refute or deny the quiet voice of the inner soul speaking with personal conviction?[3]

If you are struggling with doubts and concerns I have always found it useful to return to core of what you absolutely know to be true and then trust in Heavenly Father to guide you.

Do you believe God will answer prayers?
Do you believe you are a child of God?
Do you believe Jesus Christ is the Savior?
Do you believe Joseph Smith was a prophet?
Do you believe in the Book of Mormon?

These are examples of basic questions that will be anchors in times of doubt. Once we remember what we know to be true, we can build upon it to strengthen our testimony about the things we have not yet learned.

My wife, Holly, is a convert to the Church. When she was investigating the Church she had many good questions. Little by little they were answered, but there were still some questions that she had.

One day she surprised me and told me she was ready to be baptized. I asked her about her questions. She told me that she still had them. But she was given an answer that helped her know what to do. The answer to her prayers was that she would always have questions, but if she followed the Lord first, the answers would always come. She has testified to me on several occasions that this continues to be true.

Heavenly Father will never lead you astray if you seek Him humbly and in sincerity. And if you are unsure about something, follow the principles and suggestions outlined in this book in chapter three. This is the pattern revealed by Heavenly Father and His authorized servants. Trust that Heavenly Father will answer you. He will.

The Savior promised those who received the basic principles would be given more. (See Mark 4:24–25; see especially the JST footnote)

In what has come to be known as the King Follet discourse, Joseph Smith talked about the learning of eternal truths. He stated:

> When you climb a ladder, you must begin at the bottom, and ascend step by step, until you arrive at the top; and so it is with the principles of the Gospel—you must begin with the first, and go on until you learn all the principles of exaltation. But it will be a great while after you have passed through the veil before you will have learned them. It is not all be comprehended in this world; it will be a great work to learn our salvation and exaltation even beyond the grave."[4]

It is reasonable to have questions while in mortality. If you look carefully at the scriptures you will see that many great revelations have come to us because of specific questions.

The same will happen to you if you seek answers in the right way.

Notes

1. Howard W. Hunter, in Conference Report, October 1960, 108.
2. John K. Carmack, "The Soil and Roots of Testimony," *Ensign,* November 1988, 25.
3. Gordon B. Hinckely, "Testimony," *Ensign,* May 1998, 69.
4. Smith, Joseph. *Teachings of the Prophet Joseph Smith.* Selected by Joseph Fielding Smith. (Salt Lake City: Deseret Book, 1976), 348.

Chapter 5
Bearing Testimony

To bear means to bring forward. The scriptures and brethren have been very clear on the subject of how to bear or bring forward your testimony. But it seems to be a lesson that continues to be missed by many.

From Elder Russell Ballard we read,

> My experience throughout the Church leads me to worry that too many of our members linger on "I am thankful" and "I love," and too few are able to say with humble but sincere clarity, "I know." As a result, our meetings sometimes lack the testimony-rich, spiritual underpinnings that stir the soul and have meaningful, positive impact on the lives of all who hear them."
>
> Our testimony meetings need to be more centered on the Savior, the doctrines of the gospel, the blessings of the restoration, and the teachings of the scriptures. We need to replace stories, travelogues, and lectures with pure testimonies. Those who are entrusted to speak and teach in our meetings need to do so with doctrinal power that will be both heard and felt, lifting the spirits and edifying our people.[1]

Bearing a testimony is neither an opportunity to confess our sins publicly nor to find fault with one another.

A few years ago I brought a friend to church. His first visit happened to be a fast and testimony meeting. I really didn't think too much of this typical testimony meeting until after, when he asked me what had just happened. He said he heard us continually talking about how thankful everyone was for the Church and how we knew that the Church was true but he didn't know why or what it meant. He could recite back to me anecdotes and stories that were shared in the meeting but he said he felt far from edified.

Elder Dallin H. Oaks wrote of a letter he received that had a similar experience:

> I quote from a recent letter I received from a member in the United States. He described what he heard in a fast and testimony meeting: "I sat and listened to seventeen testimonies and never heard Jesus mentioned or referred to in any way. I thought I might be in [some other denomination], but I supposed not because there were no references to God, either.... The following Sunday, I again attended church. I sat through a priesthood lesson, a Gospel doctrine lesson, and seven sacrament meeting speakers and never once heard the name of Jesus or any reference to him."
>
> Perhaps that description is exaggerated. Surely, it is exceptional. I quote it because it provides a vivid reminder for all of us.[2]

Too often testimony bearing is taken lightly and in the process of bearing testimony we forget to testify. We must not forget that it is a sacred privilege. While it may be necessary to share some details of an experience or situation relevant to our testimony, we must be cautious that we do not let it overshadow the message of the testimony itself, which is to be focused on the gospel principles and the mission of Jesus

Christ. Too many details dilute the spiritual impact of a testimony. Keep your testimony brief and to the point.

The Doctrine and Covenants gives some additional counsel to guide those who would teach or bear testimony. "And of tenets thou shalt not talk, but thou shalt declare repentance and faith on the Savior, and remission of sins by baptism, and by fire, yea, even the Holy Ghost" (D&C 19:31).

"Tenets" are considered opinions or irrelevant principles. We are commanded to leave tenets alone and focus on the basic doctrines of the gospel.

As I have carefully studied the scriptures and talks of the brethren, there are certain things that appear again and again as appropriate truths to testify of. The testimonies found in these sources:

Testify that God is our Father
Testify that Jesus is the Christ
Testify of the Atonement
Testify of the plan of salvation
Testify of blessing that follow obedience to the gospel
Testify of the truth of basic gospel principles
Testify of the power of prayer
Testify of the restoration of the gospel
Testify of the mission of Joseph Smith
Testify of the Book of Mormon
Testify of the authority of God in the Church today
Testify of the living Prophet
Testify of how a testimony is gained

In the scriptures, words of the brethren, and other Church resources I find no speculation, opinions, or unrelated stories. I find testimony. And I find it clearly. And where testimony is clear there is great power. These are the things we need to teach each other. These are things that will edify us. These are examples for each of us to follow.

It is also interesting to note that the brethren are very careful when speaking of sacred spiritual experiences. When we bear our testimonies we should also be careful not to cast our most sacred pearls on display. "Remember that that which cometh from above is sacred, and must be spoken with care, and by constraint of the Spirit" (D&C 63:64). For example, sharing personal things from a patriarchal blessing is probably not in keeping with this counsel.

Some additional thoughts to share are in regards to clarity with the language which we use to bear our testimony. Avoid words that investigators, non-members, and children do not understand. A testimony should also avoid flowery language.

A testimony is a sacred gift and not a parade of intellectual sophistry. Testimony must be done with an eye single to the glory of God. If we bear testimony to be seen of men we have our reward.

There is another warning that is important to mention. This consideration comes from President Spencer W. Kimball. He stated,

> "You are there to bear your own witness. It is amazing what you can say in 60 seconds by way of testimony, or 120, or 240, or whatever time you are given, if you confine yourselves to testimony."[3]

Keeping our testimonies brief also demonstrates consideration for others who may wish to share their testimonies. In a First Presidency letter dated May 2, 2002, we read,

> We are concerned that in some instances, members who desire to bear their testimonies in fast and testimony meeting do not have the opportunity to do so. Bishoprics are encouraged to help all people learn to express a brief,

heartfelt testimony of the Savior, His teachings, and the Restoration, so that more members may have the opportunity to participate.[4]

We should also avoid bearing testimony out of habit. It is not obligatory to bear testimony every month. When something becomes commonplace its sacredness becomes diminished. We should also recognize that this habit may rob others of their desires to share their testimonies.

When we bear testimony clearly, boldly, and with conviction, the Holy Ghost will witness to the truth of what we testify. When the Spirit stands with us in testimony miracles can happen, hearts can be touched, and souls can be converted.

I was impressed with a statement by Elder Bruce R. McConkie at the beginning of one of his talks. He opened his remarks by saying, "I desire to bear testimony to myself, to you as members of the Church, and to all the world."[5] I have found it interesting that he shares who is affected by his testimony in this order.

Myself—As we bear testimony we immediately affect ourselves. Our personal conviction grows and the Holy Ghost strengthens us individually.

Members of the Church—Our testimony next blesses those who hear us and are receptive to the Spirit. Often these are members of the Church.

All the world—Our testimony goes into the world, either by our own voice or through those we may touch.

Do we realize the lasting effect that a powerful testimony may have? Is not this also the way that our Father also carries out his work?

> Wherefore, by the ministering of angels, and by every word which proceeded forth out of the mouth of God, men began to exercise faith in Christ; and thus by faith, they did lay hold upon every good thing; and thus it was until the coming of Christ...
>
> Neither have angels ceased to minister unto the children of men. For behold, they are subject unto him, [God] to minister according to the word of his command, showing themselves unto them of strong faith and a firm mind in every form of godliness.
>
> And the office of their [the angels] ministry is to call men unto repentance, and to fulfil and to do the work of the covenants of the Father, which he hath made unto the children of men, to prepare the way among the children of men, by declaring the word of Christ unto the chosen vessels of the Lord, that they may bear testimony of him.
>
> And by so doing, the Lord God prepareth the way that the residue of men may have faith in Christ, that the Holy Ghost may have place in their hearts, according to the power thereof; and after this manner bringeth to pass the Father, the covenants which he hath made unto the children of men. (Moroni 7:25, 29–32)

This is the pattern by which God reveals truth to the world. God speaks to angels, angels reveal it to the chosen vessels of the Lord, and those people in turn reveal these truths to the world. This gospel is taught by testimony.

Bearing your testimony is also done in ways other than sharing it aloud. A person's testimony can be seen by their actions.

Valiant in Testimony

Testimony is found in how we live our lives, and those who are valiant in the testimony of Jesus Christ will receive immeasurable rewards. "All thrones and dominions, principalities and powers, shall be revealed and set forth upon all who have endured valiantly for the gospel of Jesus Christ" (D&C 121:29).

Those who are less valiant will not receive the same reward. Speaking of those in the terrestrial kingdom, the Lord stated: "These are they who are not valiant in the testimony of Jesus; wherefore, they obtain not the crown over the kingdom of our God" (D&C 76:79).

Elder Bruce R. McConkie expressed an important truth when he said, "Members of the Church who have testimonies and who live clean and upright lives, but who are not courageous and valiant, do not gain the celestial kingdom."[6]

Elder McConkie also gave some insight as to what it means to be valiant in the testimony of Jesus.

> To be valiant in the testimony of Jesus is to take the Lord's side on every issue. It is to vote as he would vote. It is to think what he thinks, to believe what he believes, to say what he would say and do what he would do in the same the situation. It is to have the mind of Christ and be one with him as he is one with his Father.[7]

Rather than lay down our lives physically for our testimony as many martyrs have done, we are required to give lives of service and obedience.

Our lives of testimony will serve to lift and strengthen others and ourselves. It is important to remember that although we may know the gospel is true, we will not be blessed to inherit Celestial glory unless we are true and our lives bear that witness also.

How to Listen to a Testimony

How we listen to a testimony is just as important as how we bear one. For when a testimony is borne by the Spirit, both the bearer and the hearer are blessed.

In Doctrine and Covenants 50 we read,

> Wherefore, he that preacheth and he that receiveth, understand one another, and both are edified and rejoice together. And that which doth not edify is not of God, and is darkness.
>
> That which is of God is light; and he that receiveth light, and continueth in God, receiveth more light; and that light groweth brighter and brighter until the perfect day. (D&C 50:22–24)

There are many things we can learn if we listen carefully as others bear their testimony. Often we will learn more from the whisperings of the Spirit than we will from the words which are spoken. President Kimball stated,

> Testimony meetings are some of the best meetings in the ward in the whole month, if you have the spirit. *If you are bored at a testimony meeting, there is something the matter with you, and not the other people.* You can get up and bear your testimony and you think it is the best meeting in the month; but if you sit there and count the grammatical errors and laugh at the man who can't speak very well, you'll be bored, and on that board you'll slip right out of the Kingdom. Don't forget it! You have to *fight* for a testimony. You have to *keep* fighting![8] (emphasis added)

Although children may not have the knowledge or the vocabulary to express their feelings, we need to understand that they also may be touched by the Spirit to declare the things which they "have heard, and verily believe, and know to be true" (D&C 80:4). Allowing them to bear their testimonies is a powerful way in which they will grow.

It is thought by some that silence in a testimony meeting is wasted time. I have heard that comment made a few times in meetings I have been in. This is not true. Even quiet times in a testimony meeting can be moments of worship that allow us to reflect on the feelings of the Spirit. Concern that time is going to waste away is not a proper motive for bearing testimony.

Listening carefully to others bear testimony strengthens us and creates a bond of unity. It strengthens our sense of brother and sisterhood and is a means of enjoying spiritual experiences together.

When we are unified the intensity of the Spirit will grow. Listening attentively and praying for the Spirit to sustain the individual bearing testimony brings unity. This is the unity the Savior spoke of in the Doctrine and Covenants:

> Verily, verily, I say unto you, as I said unto my disciples, where two or three are gathered together in my name, as touching one thing, behold, there will I be in the midst of them—even so am I in the midst of you. (D&C 6:32)

Notes

1. M. Russell Ballard, "Pure Testimony," *Ensign,* November 2004, 40.
2. Dallin H. Oakes, "Witnesses of Christ," *Ensign,* November 1990, 29.
3. Spencer W. Kimball, "President Kimball Speaks Out on Testimony," *New Era,* August 1981, 4.
4. First Presidency Letter, May 2, 2002.
5. Bruce R. McConkie, "The Testimony of Jesus," *Ensign,* July 1972, 109.
6. Bruce R. McConkie, "Be Valiant in the Fight of Faith," *Ensign,* November 1974, 33.

7. ibid, 33.
8. Spencer W. Kimball, "President Kimball Speaks Out on Testimony," *New Era,* August 1981, 4.

Chapter 6

How to Lose Your Testimony

I hope that we can pay careful attention to the warnings in this section, for the consequences are terrible. President Harold B. Lee warned,

> Testimony isn't something you have today, and you are going to have always. A testimony is fragile. It is as hard to hold as a moonbeam. It is something you have to recapture every day of your life.[1]

Testimony is a gift. When the gift is not appreciated it will be taken away. The Savior warned, "For he that receiveth, to him shall be given: and he that recieveth not, from him shall be taken even that which he hath" (Mark 4:25; see also the JST footnote).

My mission president spoke once of the process of losing your testimony. He used the example of how when we sit close to a campfire everything looks bright. When we turn our eyes away out into the darkness, the darkness becomes even darker than before. In order to maintain a strong testimony we must keep focused on the brightness of the fire.

Elder Joseph B. Wirthlin said about the fire of testimony:

> Unfortunately, some in the Church may believe sincerely that their testimony is a raging bonfire when it really is little more than the faint flickering of a candle. Their faithfulness has more to do with habit than holiness, and their pursuit of personal righteousness almost always takes a back seat to their pursuit of personal interests and pleasure. With such a feeble light of testimony for protection, these travelers on life's highways are easy prey for the wolves of the adversary.[2]

Just as a fire must be fed to burn properly, a testimony also must be tended. How is the fire of testimony kept strong?

Elder Donald L. Staheli of the Seventy made some powerful observations.

> Daily fervent prayers seeking forgiveness and special help and direction are essential to our lives and the nourishment of our testimonies. When we become hurried, repetitive, casual, or forgetful in our prayers, we tend to lose the closeness of the Spirit, which is so essential in the continual direction we need to successfully manage the challenges of our everyday lives. Family prayer every morning and night adds additional blessings and power to our individual prayers and to our testimonies.[3]

Elder Charles Didier of the Seventy also adds,

> If you follow the steps to obtain a testimony, you do exactly the opposite to deny it or lose it. Do not pray; the door to revelation will be closed. Do not be humble but listen to your own superior voice. Do not participate in the ordinances of the gospel but follow the practices of the world. Do not follow Church leaders but

> be critical of them. Do not listen to prophets and follow their counsel but interpret their declarations according to your own desires. Do not obey the commandments but live according to your own appetites and desires.[4]

Testimony is kept by doing the gospel basics. Keeping a testimony is not a hard thing to do if we will do our duty.

Testimony also must be borne. A fire that is not allowed to breathe, even if it has sufficient fuel, will eventually fizzle out. If one of the elements of gaining a testimony is to bear it then how do expect to kept, if we will not bear it? (See Elder Packer's remarks on finding a testimony through bearing it in the chapter on gaining a testimony.)

As a testimony is shared it becomes stronger and stronger, and as a fire it will have the power to ignite and affect others around you.

NOTES

1. Church News, July 15, 1972, 4.
2. Joseph B. Wirthlin, "Spiritual Bonfires of Testimony," *Ensign,* November 1992, 34.
3. Donald L. Staheli, "Securing Our Testimonies," *Ensign,* November 2004, 37.
4. Charles Didier, "Testimony," *Ensign,* November 1991, 62.

Chapter 7

A Promise

When we have testimony and do our duty, it cannot be taken from us. One of the most comforting promises that I have found in regards to keeping your testimony comes from Elder Richard G. Scott. Elder Scott promises that Satan

> "cannot take away any blessing that has been earned.... He cannot quench true faith. He cannot take away your testimony. Yes, these things can be lost by succumbing to his temptations. But he has no power in and of himself to destroy them."[1] (emphasis added)

A testimony is our greatest blessing and it can burn within us if we care for it properly. When a testimony is strong, it will burn away doubts and fears. It will light our path and the way of those around us. If we nurture it, it will grow until it is as brilliant as the perfect day.

The Blessings of a Testimony

Through this book I hope you have been able to recognize many of the blessings that come from a testimony.

A testimony is a gift directly from divinity. It is precious and sacred. Elder Robert D. Hales spoke of some of the gifts that come as a result of living a life with a strong testimony. He stated,

> Those lifted by the power of testimony can find greater happiness and fidelity in marriage. Their testimonies are an antidote to the plague of divorce. They enjoy greater freedom, seldom enslaved to alcohol, tobacco, drugs, abuse, and other forms of self-indulgence. They find strength to deal with the problems of life.[2]

The scriptures and words of the brethren contain many blessings that accompany a life of testimony. Having a testimony will:

Allow us to know God lives.
Give us a witness of the divinity of Jesus Christ.
Teach us of the reality of the Atonement.
Confirm the truthfulness of the Book of Mormon.
Uphold the calling of Joseph Smith.
Tell us there is a prophet on the earth today.
Bless us with an increased desire be obedient to the gospel.
Help us overcome temptation.
Bring more unity into our marriages, families, and wards.
Develop a spirit of forgiveness and charity.
Bless us with a desire to repent.
Teach us line upon line.
Help us become converted.

Testimony is a necessary principle of the gospel. As you follow the path that leads to testimony all of the blessings outlined here will be yours. Testimony is carefully obtained and carefully maintained. It is my witness that as you carefully develop your testimony you will come to know the Savior personally. And that brings us to the last blessing…

A testimony will bring eternal life.

Notes

1. Richard G. Scott, "The Power of a Strong Testimony," *Ensign,* November 2001, 87.
2. Robert D. Hales, "The Importance of Receiving a Personal Testimony," *Ensign,* November 1994, 20.

Chapter 8
Some Thoughts from the Prophets

Joseph Smith

"The fundamental principles of our religion are the testimony of the Apostles and Prophets, concerning Jesus Christ, that He died, was buried, and rose again the third day, and ascended into heaven; and all other things which pertain to our religion are only appendages to it."[1]

Brigham Young

"If all the talent, tact, wisdom, and refinement of the world had been combined in one individual, and that person had been sent to me with the Book of Mormon, and had declared in the most exalted of earthly eloquence, the truth of it, undertaking to prove it by his learning and worldly wisdom, it would have been to me like the smoke which arises only to vanish. But when I saw a man without eloquence, or talents for public speaking, who could only just say, 'I know by the power of the Holy Ghost that the Book of Mormon is true, that Joseph Smith is a prophet of the Lord,' [the]

Holy Ghost proceeding from that individual illuminate[d] my understanding, and light, glory, and immortality [were] before me."[2]

David O. McKay

"There is nothing which a man can possess in this world, which will bring more comfort, more hope and faith than a testimony of the existence of a Heavenly Father who loves us, or of the reality of Jesus Christ, his Only Begotten Son, that those two heavenly personages appeared to the Prophet Joseph and established the Church of Jesus Christ, and that men are officially authorized to represent Deity."[3]

"A testimony of the gospel of Jesus Christ is the most sacred, the most precious gift in our lives, obtained only by adherence to the principles of the gospel, not by following the paths of the world. You may get momentary pleasures by following the enticements of the world.

"You may get transitory pleasure, yes; but you cannot find joy—you cannot find happiness. Happiness is found only along that well-beaten track, narrow as it is, though strait, which leads to life eternal."[4]

"This testimony has been revealed to every sincere man and woman who has conformed to the principles of the Gospel of Jesus Christ, who has obeyed the ordinances, and has become entitled to and has received the Spirit of God, the Holy Ghost, to guide him."[5]

Joseph F. Smith

"Every person should know that the gospel is true, as this is everyone's privilege who is baptized and receives the Holy Ghost.... I know that the gospel is true, and that God is with his people; and that if I will do my duty and keep his commandments, the clouds will roll by, and the mists will disappear."[6]

Joseph Fielding Smith

" A testimony of the gospel is a convincing knowledge given by revelation to the individual who humbly seeks the truth."[7]

Harold B. Lee

"The real strength of the Church is to be measured by the individual testimonies to be found in the total membership of The Church of Jesus Christ of Latter-day Saints."[8]

Spencer W. Kimball

"To hold his testimony one must bear it often and live worthy of it."[9]

Ezra Taft Benson

"A testimony is one of the few possessions we may take with us when we leave this life.... A testimony of Jesus means that you accept the divine mission of Jesus Christ, embrace His gospel, and do His works; it means you accept the prophetic mission of Joseph Smith and his successors."[10]

Gordon B. Hinckley

Personal testimony is the factor which turns people around in their living as they come into this Church. This is the element which motivates the membership to forsake all in the service of the Lord. This is the quiet, encouraging voice which sustains without pause those who walk in faith down to the last days of their lives."[11]

Notes

1. Smith, Joseph. *Teachings of the Prophet Joseph Smith.* Selected by Joseph Fielding Smith. (Salt Lake City: Deseret Book, 1976), 121.
2. Young, Brigham. *Teachings of the Presidents of the Church: Brigham Young.* (Salt Lake City: The Church of Jesus Christ of Latter-day Saints, 1997), 315.
3. David O. McKay, in Conference Report, October 1953, 88.
4. McKay, David O. *Treasures of Life,* compiled by Clare M. Middlemiss. (Salt Lake City: Deseret Book, 1962), 229.
5. McKay, David O. *Pathways to Happiness.* (Salt Lake City: Bookcraft, 1975), 314–15.
6. Smith, Joseph Fielding. *Gospel Doctrine: Selections from Sermons and Writings of Joseph F. Smith.* (Salt Lake City: Deseret Book, 1971), 43.
7. Smith, Joseph Fielding. *Answers to Gospel Questions.* Compiled by Joseph Fielding Smith Jr. (5 vols., Salt Lake City: Deseret Book, 1957–1966) 3:31.
8. Harold B. Lee, "Strengthen the Stakes of Zion," *Ensign,* July 1973, 6.
9. Spencer W. Kimball, in Conference Report, October 1944., 45.
10. Ezra Taft Benson, "Valiant in the Testimony of Jesus," *Ensign,* May 1982, 62.
11. Gordon B. Hinckley, "Testimony," *Ensign,* May 1998, 69.

About the Author

Douglas J. Vermeeren

Douglas Vermeeren has taught the gospel as a full-time missionary in Belgium, a Seminary teacher, a gospel doctrine instructor, and a gospel principles instructor. Doug has also taught English classes in China. While in China he developed a program for Chinese university teachers that helped them to be more effective instructors of English. He was also selected as the first foreign teacher to speak at a teacher's day conference for Chinese political and educational leaders for the province of Shanxi.

Doug was a featured speaker at Ricks College's (now BYUI) Issues and Interactions symposium (speaking on the Garden of Gethsemane) and was Ricks College's first student Academic lecturer speaking on the Book of Abraham.

He has written articles for the *Ensign, New Era,* and the *Friend.* One of his articles in the *Friend* was published in more than 22 languages worldwide.

Doug loves to teach and talk about the gospel, especially early Church history. He has a strong testimony of the gospel and of the Saviour Jesus Christ.

Doug and his wife, Holly, live in Calgary, Alberta, Canada, with their three children, Julienne, Jordan, and Jared.

0 26575 79967 5